Labyri.

AN INTRODUCTION TO THE HOW, WHAT, AND WHY OF LABYRINTHS AND LABYRINTH WALKING

Clive Johnson

labyrinthe

Copyright © 2017 by Clive Johnson.

First published March 2017.

All rights reserved. No part of this publication may be reproduced, distributed or transmitted in any form or by any means, including photocopying, recording, or other electronic or mechanical methods, without the prior written permission of the publisher, except in the case of brief quotations embodied in critical reviews and certain other noncommercial uses permitted by copyright law.

Labyrinthe Press
Leigh-on-Sea, United Kingdom
www.labyrinthepublishers.com

Book Layout©2017 BookDesignTemplates.com
Cover illustration ©iStock, mammuth/Peter-Zelei
Other illustrations © sfermin
Distributed by Ingram

British Library Cataloguing in Publication Data
Labyrinth Alpha–Omega/Clive Johnson. –1st ed.
ISBN 978-0-9957351-0-1 (print edition)
ISBN 978-0-9957351-1-8 (electronic edition)

Also available as an Audible digital audiobook.

Paperback and ebook editions of this book are also available in Spanish./ Libros en rústica y libros electrónicos de este libro también están disponibles en español.

Quantity sales. Special discounts are available on quantity purchases of this book. For details, please contact info@labyrinthepublishers.com.

Contents

Preface 1
Introduction 5
The Labyrinth through Time 9
Why the Labyrinth? 23
How to Approach the Labyrinth? 49
Where Next for your Labyrinth Journey? . 61
Notes and References 69
Bibliography 73
The Labyrinth Resources Guide 79

Preface

THE NOTION OF EMBARKING on a 10,000 mile road trip might seem crazy by most people's standards. To undertake such a journey while hauling a large, rolled-up stretch of canvas might seem like an insanity, especially when accompanied with an idea that it will be possible to persuade strangers along the way to not only open up their doors and allow this strangely painted mat to be spread across their floors, but also to welcome in anyone who wants to walk it who might happen to be passing by.

I must confess, that I've had many doubts about launching such a project. For one thing, the idea came to me quite suddenly, following an inspiring meeting of The Labyrinth Society, a community of several hundred people who are fanatical about discovering, making, collecting, and walking labyrinths.

I barely thought about the challenges involved, let alone the cost or the time that such an expedition would take. But I'm a nomad by nature, and like to think that I follow the leading of my heart – taking my cue from the one whom I call 'The Great Divine'.

So, with a minimum of planning and yearning to make this project happen, I set about organizing my first night's stay, took a deep breath, and committed more than $2,000 of my savings to have a labyrinth made.

The passion that drove me, along with that which inspires the growing number of labyrinth aficionados who form the core of The Labyrinth Society's membership, is something that's hard to put into words.

Labyrinths have a magical appeal – to walk one is not just to take a leisurely stride, as you might do when walking a dog. All manner of emotions can come to the surface when stepping onto the labyrinth's path – along with fresh ideas, meaningful reflections, and inspirations for courses of action that you might take when you step back outside again.

The labyrinth is an ancient archetype, a secret known to our ancestors across many centuries. To walk one requires no qualification or previous experience. Young and old (and those somewhere in between); rich and poor; Hispanic, Native American, and Anglo-Saxon; Jew, Muslim, Christian, and Hindu; able-bodied and physically challenged; atheist and agnostic; city-folk and country-kind – the labyrinth invites anyone and everyone to step into its path, without judgment, and treating everyone as an equal.

"No other tool can so successfully bring into alignment the many aspects of our being and teach us so clearly that we are all on the same path," claims Helen Curry, a former president of The Labyrinth Society [1]. "Nothing else seems to speak so effectively to people of different religions and cultural backgrounds".

Perhaps this is one of the reasons why labyrinth walking has become so popular during recent years – while each person's walk is unique and made in their own time and way, the labyrinth is accepting and embracing of all.

The fact that it does embrace the beautiful diversity of humanity is one reason why I'm drawn to it, but so too is its ability to transcend any affiliation to a particular religion or other system of belief. It is truly interfaith in its offering, and equally welcoming for people of no faith or having a particular point of view about 'spiritual' matters.

In this short book, I'll say a little about why I believe the labyrinth has such power. We'll take a brief tour of our own – stopping off at various places and times in history to see how labyrinths have been used by different cultures, before returning to the current day, to try to make sense of its relevance for us in the here and now.

We'll consider how labyrinths have been used to help people face different situations in their lives – including for healing, reconciliation, and in bringing communities together. This brief survey of uses will neatly dovetail with a reflection on why labyrinths have such an appeal for so many people.

We'll explore what you might expect to experience when you start walking, and offer some thoughts on how you might want to approach a labyrinth before a walk.

To this end, we'll end our tour by looking at some of the options available for discovering more about, and finding opportunities to experience labyrinth walking in your locality and elsewhere – either on a group or community basis, or privately, under your own steam.

The final section of the book provides a directory of books, journals, podcasts, website links, and 'how to' videos to help you explore and enjoy labyrinths further – including the possibility of bringing one into your own home, organization, or community.

Introduction

I FIRST WALKED a labyrinth barely ten years ago. I'd been attracted to a small classified advert in the back pages of an events listing magazine, inviting newcomers to a candlelit labyrinth walk that was taking place in a church close to where I then lived.

The fact that this particular walk was taking place in a church is not especially significant – as I later discovered when I became a regular walker along with others who'd stumbled upon the labyrinth during that and similar evenings, many of whom considered themselves to be anything but religious. But the stunning Gothic architecture of this high parish church in a residential quarter of Brighton and Hove on England's south coast, combined with subtle lighting and atmospheric live music, didn't fail to impress me.

The wide nave of the church had been cleared of its chairs to make space for the large canvas sheet on which the labyrinth was painted. 112 candles flickered around the circular boundary of the labyrinth itself, whose path was picked out on the canvas in a calming royal blue. This giant creation faithfully reproduced the pattern and measurements of the famous labyrinth that can be found in Chartres Cathedral in France.

It was itself inspired by a similar canvas labyrinth that used to be regularly laid out at Grace Cathedral in San Francisco – one of the earliest examples of a portable labyrinth that was brought into a modern public space. The canvas labyrinth at Grace Cathedral has now been replaced with a permanent one, which is set into the cathedral's floor – testifying to the popularity of the original.

My walk was introduced by a kindly gentleman with a beaming smile and paternal aura (who has since become a very good friend). The event's facilitator gave a brief outline of the history of labyrinths, before offering some guidelines for walking. After dimming the lights, our host signaled the opening of the labyrinth by brushing together the cymbals of a Tibetan Chime, and then one by one–although not in a rush–individuals stepped forward to take their place at the entrance to the wide canvas.

Labyrinth A-Ω

I bided my time, waiting some twenty minutes or more before feeling ready to start my walk. I've since discovered that this sense of when to make a move is usually replicated for me in the labyrinth itself – sometimes I feel an impulse to move at a pace, at other times to move very slowly, if at all.

Taking my first step onto a labyrinth's path felt like stepping over a threshold. Once on the path, I had a sense of being detached from what might be happening outside – my concerns were limited to walking and breathing, knowing that nothing more was expected of me.

This idea of being in a different space when inside the labyrinth is emphasized by the labyrinth scholar Hermann Kern, who remarks: "What is important is that the outer line [of the labyrinth] clearly separates the exterior from the inner space" [2]. This inner space is a place where we can connect with our inner lives.

I don't now remember very much about that first walk. I know that I eventually arrived at the center– and not that it would have mattered had I not–and that I spent a little time there crouching on the canvas while others circled around me. There were a lot of people walking that day, some stepping by me during my walk, others coming toward me from the opposite direction, and still others in my peripheral vision coming and going, as they appeared and disappeared on their journeys along the labyrinth's winding path.

When I finished walking, I returned to my seat and allowed myself time to process the experience that I'd just enjoyed. I felt at peace, uplifted, and very comfortable with the place that I had come to. I may have jotted down a few thoughts that had come to me during my walk – I can't remember now, but this wouldn't have been unusual (it's not a bad idea to have a notebook handy when you finish a labyrinth walk, in case flashes of inspiration or fresh insights come to you, as they often do).

I knew that I didn't want to make this labyrinth walk a one-off experience. Fortunately for me, the church hosted a regular breakfast walk, albeit using a smaller labyrinth. I became a regular at these early morning walks, and soon built firm friendships with the loyal band of fellow walkers who joined with me for coffee and croissants after our walking. Some of us occasionally extended our practice, taking a very slow, meditative walk toward the beach, which lay just a few blocks to the south of the church.

A trip to Chartres followed some years later. Here, at specific times, it's still possible to walk the same 270 or so stones that mark the labyrinth's path in the cathedral's floor. In doing so, it's humbling to consider the countless visitors who've trod this same path since the thirteenth century CE.

CHAPTER 1

The Labyrinth through Time

THE LABYRINTH AT CHARTRES is particularly well-known, perhaps because the cathedral was for many centuries an important destination for pilgrims. Visitors included those who were unable to journey to Jerusalem; the labyrinth instead offering a symbolic focus for a pilgrimage.

Many are said to have even walked the cold stone tiles on their knees, often following long and arduous journeys to reach the hallowed town, with its imposing cathedral looming into view many miles before they reached their destination. For a pilgrim, to reach the center of the labyrinth at such a great cathedral was to arrive at the New Jerusalem.

The design of the Chartres labyrinth is strikingly beautiful. Set into the pattern are 112 lunations, or ornamental motifs that mark the labyrinth's outer-border. With near perfect symmetry, the labyrinth is as much a testimony to the grandeur and masterwork of this outstanding cathedral, as are the many stained glass windows that shine into its great space, including the exceptional rose windows that bathe the north and south transepts, and the intricately crafted sculptures that adorn its exterior.

It's often said that the great rose window at the western end of the nave would transpose exactly onto the plan of the labyrinth were it able to be levered from its vertical plane onto the floor of the cathedral, however the eminent labyrinth researcher Jeff Saward has disproved this theory [3]. Nevertheless, mysteries about the meaning of the labyrinth's design continue to engage scholars, some speculating that it may once have provided a space for playing a ball game, others suggesting that it may have been used as an elaborate calendar.

Other remarkable examples of sacred geometry are to be found in this space, but few are as elegantly proportioned as the labyrinth [4]. The gothic masterpiece at Chartres is one of a number of cathedrals, abbeys, and prominent churches surviving from the medieval period in Europe that are home to a labyrinth. Other examples include the labyrinths at Amiens, Poitiers, and Saint-Quentin (others are known to have existed, but have since been destroyed).

Labyrinth A-Ω

Chartres Cathedral, home to the best known labyrinth from the medieval period

Elsewhere in Europe, labyrinths can be found in alternative settings, and—as far as we can tell—were used for differing purposes.

Around the coast of Scandinavia and in Northern Germany, for example, as many as 700 stone-marked labyrinths have been found at settlements that have become known as 'Troy Towns', since these structures closely model labyrinth patterns found on Cretan prints in which young men would reenact a Trojan battle.

The excavations in Scandinavia all follow a similar, although alternative pattern to the classical design. The Scandinavian variant is now commonly known as the 'Baltic Wheel' style. Their proximity to the coast suggests that they were important gathering places for fisherfolk.

It's conjectured that the men from the villages would gather at the labyrinth to pray or to perform a ritual before putting out to sea. Prayers would be offered for their protection, and the gathered would petition their god for a bountiful catch. Perhaps too, some of the men may have walked the labyrinth before setting out into dangerous waters. We can only imagine what thoughts might have been running through their minds as they did so, and what burdens they may have carried in their hearts.

On the far side of the continent, in the islands and territories where the Greeks had dominion, other examples of labyrinths, either real or written about or painted on pottery finds, abound. Undoubtedly, the most famous of these is the labyrinth at the Palace of Knossos on the island of Crete (although this is a labyrinth that may be known to mythology, however hasn't yet been confirmed by any physical evidence). As you may know, the famous tale from Greek mythology tells the story of the Athenian Theseus, who with the help of a sword and a ball of thread gifted to him by the lovestruck daughter of the Cretan King Minos, Ariadne, manages to overcome a fearsome monster that's trapped at the center of a supposedly inescapable labyrinth. After defeating the Minotaur, Theseus retraces his steps by following the thread that has unraveled on his inward journey, the other end of which was still held onto by Ariadne. The pair then flee to the island of Naxos, leaving Minos in a fury, and vowing to punish the labyrinth's creator.

Classical, medieval and Baltic labyrinth styles

This labyrinth was designed by Daedalus, an ingenious inventor, as a means for housing the Minotaur, which Minos was ashamed to present as his son. Each year, seven young men and seven young women were sent from the mainland as an offering to satisfy the Minotaur's insatiable appetite. Following Theseus' solving of the labyrinth's riddle and overpowering the Minotaur, Daedalus made to flee Minos' kingdom, but the furious king banished him to an impregnable tower as a punishment for his supposed assistance for Theseus. We encounter him again in the story involving his son Icarus, who famously flew too close to the sun, causing the melting of the wax seal in the wings that his father had made for him as a means for escaping their imprisonment in the tower.

Daedalus' 'labyrinth' may be what we now call a 'maze'. It may have included many dead ends and crossroads, designed to keep the Minotaur safely imprisoned at its center, as well as to trap anyone who dared to wander in. However, Theseus found the one true path–the labyrinth–which doesn't set out to ensure or fool those who tread its path. Modern puzzle mazes incorporate the same principle – for those who know their secret, there is an uncomplicated and single path to the center.

In fact, the first mention of the word 'maze' didn't appear in the English language until the fourteenth century, possibly being coined by Geoffrey Chaucer. Before then, any contained path marked out for a ceremonial purpose may have been known as a labyrinth, or rather its French or Latin equivalents, *labyrinthe* or *labyrinthum*.

The concept of a puzzle maze–or a structure that deliberately sets out to amuse and challenge with its numerous blind alleys–doesn't appear until the Elizabethan period, although various civilizations are known to have used labyrinths to ensnare or confuse an unwitting visitor.

For example, the story in the epic *Mahabharata* of Abhimanyu, son of the great Hindu warrior Arjuna, tells how the young man is taught how to make his way onto the battlefield and shown how to defeat his enemies, but not yet how to return. The tale is depicted in Hindu lore as a labyrinth, which bears a striking similarity to the Cretan style, albeit being a distinctive variant of the classical pattern.

Labyrinth A-Ω

The Hindu version, known in Sanskrit as *Chakravayu* (literally, 'wheel-battle formation'), represents the arrangement of troops in a labyrinthine pattern. It is found in numerous reliefs, as well as in Hindu, Tantric and Jain literature.

Ancient labyrinths were typically marked out in stone on the ground, or formed a motif in a floor mosaic; garden mazes with hedges appear to have been an invention of the later Renaissance period.

In contrast with a maze, a labyrinth has only one path (at least normally). Even where two or more paths are offered as a means of entry–as is the case with some specially designed labyrinths–any path that is followed leads to the labyrinth's center. This is the point: there is nothing to worry about, except to follow the path and trust that it will take you to where you need to go.

Theseus' defeat of the Minotaur is thought to have been regularly enacted by the Cretans and later by the Romans in the so-called 'crane dances' around a labyrinth, also recalling the Greeks' triumph at Troy, and so also known as the 'Game of Troy'. This gives us a further example of the uses to which labyrinths have been but – for ceremonial and celebratory purposes.

Some early Christians adapted the myth of Theseus to portray the perils of hell that face those who don't follow the single path. Their encounter with the center was to be devoured, not saved. However, it's fair to point out that Christians also believed that the labyrinth is an allegory of the soul's path toward a New Jerusalem, and that only the unfaithful could expect their journey to end with a descent into hell.

This representation of the labyrinth isn't perhaps very helpful when considering the uses that labyrinths are put to today. For one thing, we don't usually enter into a labyrinth expecting to meet a monster or having to face our demons, still less to not be able to find our way out. Demons may occasionally surface when undertaking any form of meditation, however if they do, we can be sure that facing them will be for our own good. It's true also that the labyrinth may cause us to see our shadow self–the part of us that we might not recognize as being ourselves, or want to run away from. Again, to recognize and make peace with our shadow is important if we are to grow and become fully integrated human beings.

Generally though, from the time of the Romans onward, labyrinths have been considered a space for protection. They are a safe space that holds us, even as we come into touch with our inner lives. The same is true of standing stone circles, forest groves, and circles of people – all are seen to contain a positive energy, being held by a spirit of compassion.

Happily, the labyrinths of today usually have no Minotaurs pounding the ground at their centers. Rather than being spaces that overwhelm us, they are places for discovery and growth. As Hermann Kern so aptly says: "In the labyrinth you don't lose yourself. You find yourself." [5].

Labyrinth A-Ω

The Cretan form of labyrinth (not the type that sets out to ensnare) can be seen in the pattern imprinted in the Baltic labyrinths of the Troy towns. Similar patterns have been found in labyrinths discovered in North America and India.

Examples of this pattern can be found in Jain, Hindu, and Buddhist manuscripts, as well as in physical installations that have been uncovered from as far afield as Java and Afghanistan. Such labyrinths undoubtedly predate the Christian Era, and very obviously had significance for Eastern faiths.

Still earlier labyrinths have been discovered in Egypt, such as that outlining a mortuary temple founded by Pharaoh Amenemhet III. Earlier still, one depicted on a clay tablet was found back in Knossos, which has been dated to around 1400 BCE. A slightly later example, found on a tablet excavated on the site of King Nestor's palace in Greece, is the earliest reference to a labyrinth that has been positively dated – to around 1200 BCE. However, a labyrinth painted on a rock face at Pontevedra in north-west Spain is thought to precede this by as much as 800 years, and labyrinth patterns found on three old Babylonian tablets can be dated with reasonable certainty to around the same period. Early Etruscan examples have also been found.

What is clear is that labyrinths have a very long history – perhaps as long as recorded history itself.

Unsurprisingly perhaps, the Romans took an interest in labyrinths, at least admiring them from the point of view of their artistic merit, if not for their mystical or cosmological significance. Many mosaics from the Roman period incorporate elaborate labyrinth patterns in their design, characteristically representing an angular path, which is completed in a sequence by moving from one quadrant of the floor area to another.

The Roman poet Pliny the Elder (23/24–79 CE) includes a list of labyrinths in his *Natural History*, suggesting that labyrinths had more than aesthetic appeal for the Romans (although Pliny's catalog mainly describes terrifying subterranean mazes). The importance of the labyrinth as a symbol survived in what is now Italy and elsewhere in southern Europe after the fall of the Western Roman Empire, although is far more commonly found carved into columns or cathedral walls than as a path that can be walked [6].

In the Celtic world, labyrinths seem to have played an important role. The spiraling and ascending labyrinth at Glastonbury Tor in west England is one famous example, being located at a site that is believed to have geomantic importance [7].

The Italian traveler Gernot Candolini recalls one explanation for this particular labyrinth's significance from a man that he met at this sacred place during a tour of the labyrinths of Europe: "'The

Labyrinth A-Ω

labyrinth is the belly of the mother', the man asserted, 'the umbilical cord leading to the earth'. 'It's the dance of the women', said a woman, 'and you men will never understand it'" [8]. If it's true that the labyrinth is "a symbol of the Earth, the womb of the soul, and a dancing ground", as another observer offered to Candolini during his Glastonbury visit, we can fairly say that the labyrinth has a powerful role to play in connecting us with the very ground upon which we walk, the provider of everything that we eat, and which offers us a sure base on which to build our homes – Mother Earth, or Gaia.

The history of labyrinths in the Americas remains a largely untold story. Drawings have quite recently been discovered in Brazil, Ecuador, and Peru, while mentions among Native American peoples are relatively recent. Nevertheless, a labyrinth does feature in a rock carving found at Oraibi, Arizona, dating to around 1100-1200 CE. The south-western states—notably New Mexico and Arizona—are home to the earliest references to labyrinths that have been found in North America, causing the great documentarian of labyrinths, Hermann Kern, to surmise that labyrinths had been brought there by the ancestors of the Hopi people from across the Pacific.

The concept of the labyrinth as Mother Earth, the giver of life, is seen in many Native American representations. Spiritual rebirth, and the process of passing from one world to the next, are also considered important in the labyrinth's symbolism for the Hopi people.

Notable variations to the classical pattern are found illustrated in Native American drawings and basketwork, including a square labyrinth with two entrances, and a pattern that combines both the familiar circuitous path of the classical labyrinth, along with what appears like a 'spider leg' distortion (see the diagram below).

Example of a labyrinth woven into a 1920's Pima basket, displaying an unusual variation on the classical design

The labyrinth today

So we come to the present day. It's thought that more labyrinths have been created during the past twenty years than throughout all other human history. To some extent, this might not be surprising – the world population has grown exponentially over the past hundred years or so, and of course, we have more effective means for producing portable artifacts and communicating information about them than had our ancestors.

In her book *Walking a Sacred Path*, Rev. Dr. Lauren Artress describes the unprecedented interest in the labyrinth at Grace Cathedral in San Francisco, which was first opened to the public just before New Year's Eve, 1991.

The event had been mentioned in a news article, but no one could have predicted that a queue would form outside the great cathedral on Nob Hill from 6 PM until midnight. "Opening the labyrinth to the public was like opening the floodgates of a dam," recalls Artress [9]. "There was no way of containing it; there was no going back. Things would never be the same again."

How true these words have proved to be. Such was the popularity of the labyrinth at Grace Cathedral, that Rev. Dr. Artress was soon asked to bring her ministry of labyrinth walking to many others across the United States, as well as around the world.

The great innovation with the Grace Cathedral labyrinth was the use of a portable canvas – one that could be taken from place to place, being laid out as required, and then folded away again to allow the space that it occupies to be used for other purposes. Through Lauren Artress' calling, and the earlier inspiration of New Age teacher Dr. Jean Houston, the labyrinth came to be re-established as a well-known space for healing, meditation, reflection, community building, peacemaking, and many other purposes.

Portable labyrinths can be hired out and shared among several groups or communities. The *Labyrinth Around America* initiative would not be possible without such an innovation, obviously requiring a single labyrinth that can be transported from place to place. However, permanent labyrinths have been created in many places. Some are made from stone, bricks or slate, others are made by locking together rubber mats; some are mowed into grass, others are marked out with tree stubs.

For those who are able to travel or who are fortunate to live near such places, labyrinths constructed by our ancestors can still be walked in many places – such as the giant turf labyrinth at Saffron Walden in Essex (UK), the forest labyrinth at Damme Priory in Germany, and of course, the labyrinths gracing the floors of Chartres Cathedral and other church buildings in Northern Europe.

More recent examples include the 11-circuit labyrinth that overlooks the Pacific at Land's End, in San Francisco, Labyrinth at The Edge in the Amathole Mountains of South Africa, and the installation at the University of St. Thomas in Houston, Texas. Perhaps there is a labyrinth close by your own home?

CHAPTER 2

Why the Labyrinth?

IF LABYRINTHS ARE FOUND in so many locations around the world, span a very long history, and many thousands of people have discovered a real purpose for wanting to walk them today, we might reasonably ask why labyrinths have such appeal. What exactly is the purpose of walking a labyrinth, and what happens to a person when they step onto its path?

As might already be clear from our brief potted tour of labyrinths in history, there's no single purpose that can be attributed to the labyrinth's lure. Labyrinths have variously been used for celebratory enactments (as is the case with the 'crane dances', performed to recall the victory of Theseus over the Minotaur), as a gathering place for prayer and preparation (as in the case of the Scandinavian fisherfolk that came to ask for protection on their treacherous missions), and as a path for pilgrimage (as in the case of the many pilgrims who came to the great labyrinth at Chartres and elsewhere).

Labyrinths have also been attributed as places where games have been played, sacred rituals conducted, and old enemies have come to set aside their differences.

Most significantly–and undoubtedly accounting for its popularity in modern times–for what have probably been several millennia, individuals have come to the labyrinth simply to receive its embrace, to detach from the concerns of everyday life, and just 'to be'.

The concept of 'just being' is one that's spoken about quite frequently these days, and it's easy to dismiss such a notion as being quite a quaint or even trite idea.

For me, allowing ourselves 'to be' means to stop focusing on events that have happened, and things that might happen. It means giving up any idea of having to do anything, if only for a moment – just to be conscious that we are breathing and alive. It also means being present, or actually experiencing what is happening in the moment – like noticing the sounds that may be passing by in the background, the play of the wind on our skin, or just observing how we are standing (or whatever posture we may be holding), and our connection with the ground.

'Being' means becoming aware that we inhabit a body, and that we have an inner life too. By opening our bodies to receive, and finding our core when we breathe, the labyrinth helps us make connection with this deeper life, which we might all too often give little attention to.

Curiously, when we experience what may be quite rare, fleeting moments of 'being', we seem to lose all sense of physical time; what seems like an instant may actually be much longer when we come to check out watches. Conversely, what may seem to pass over a long time might span only a few minutes on a conventional clock.

Walking often seems to bring us into a new kind of awareness – not only one in which the normal rules of time don't seem to apply, but also one in which we seem to be in a different state of being altogether.

As Lauren Artress puts it, "When we walk into the path of the labyrinth, a new world greets us. This world is not riddled with splits and divisions between mind and body. Woven within this experience is a new vision of reality" [10]. Italian labyrinth enthusiast Gernot Candolini makes a similar point: "As a person walks along, [she] learns to listen to her soul" [11].

Walking the labyrinth can involve moments like these – partly because we've taken the decision not to worry about what time is passing, but I believe also that because when we are fully mindful of being, something mystical happens. This is one of the hard to explain things that often happens during most forms of meditation (and walking a labyrinth is one way to practice meditation).

We've mentioned several other common reasons for walking labyrinths – including for receiving inspiration, assurance, and guidance. It's not uncommon to approach the labyrinth with a particular question in mind, perhaps concerning a matter that may be troubling you, or when you need to take a decision about which course to follow going forward.

Keeping a question in mind as you walk toward the labyrinth's center, but not analyzing it or tossing over different ideas in your head, it's not unusual for a fresh idea to come, or for inspiration to strike. This may not always happen during a walk, but may drop into awareness sometime later, probably when you least expect it.

Psychologists may have something to say about what is happening here, especially those who subscribe to the teachings of the great Swiss psychologist Carl Jung. Jungian followers might suggest that when a person allows themselves to detach from their usually very busy conscious thoughts, they become more sensitive to bringing into consciousness what normally exists only at a subconscious level. When we delve deep inside ourselves, they propose, we have the ability to tap into infinite wisdom – and can draw upon what's known as the collective unconscious, or the grand store of knowledge, experiences, and blueprints for life that's accessible to any human being.

Hence, if we can trust in the collective wisdom of everyone throughout history, rather than relying on our own, limited, analytical minds, it shouldn't be surprising that unexpected ideas begin to pop-up when we enter the labyrinth's embrace.

This may be the explanation offered by some psychologists, but followers of certain faith traditions might prefer to talk in terms of our being able to 'connect with the heart', or 'come into touch with God / The Divine/ The True Source', when we're able to give our egotistical mind a rest. Australian journalist and labyrinth researcher Virginia Westbury highlights "feeling, heart, connection and selfhood" as concepts that seem to underlie our current attraction to the labyrinth [12].

I don't think that it matters whose explanation may be right, and while many people's experiences may convince them one way or the other (myself included), where inspiration or guidance comes from during a meditation or labyrinth walk can't yet be empirically proven.

Still, I think it's intriguing to briefly consider the possibility of another belief that's advanced by Jungian thinkers – the notion of the archetype. Archetypes are patterns of behavior, or–if you prefer–models for living, that exist in the unconscious.

As with the concept of the collective unconscious, archetypes are a part of our extended DNA – we are born with both the ability and the tendency to tap into these timeless blueprints for life that guided our ancestors, and can guide us too. Examples include the hero, who seeks to be strong and competent; the magician, whose motto is that we create our lives from the visions we imagine; and the wise woman or man, whose life trials and maturing brings them to wholeness.

Some say that the labyrinth is an archetype itself, even if it's something that we can not only see, but walk. Perhaps it may represent 'The Great Mother', Gaia, the infinitely complex organism called Earth of which we are all living and intricately-connected living parts.

For others, the labyrinth has cosmological significance, perhaps being a model of the Cosmos itself, with its ever evolving play of life in all its diversity and apparent individual manifestations, but which are somehow connected, and which merge into one at what we might conceptualize as having a common center.

But we are getting ahead of ourselves. What the labyrinth may or may not represent really doesn't matter. We don't need to know why inspiration may come when we walk, nor why we might feel at peace or seemingly detached from worldly time. We just need to trust that the labyrinth will work its magic – and simply 'be'.

One of the labyrinth's beauties is that no one knows how it originally came to be, why it is found in so many diverse parts of the world, nor why so many people come upon wonderful experiences when walking it. When we approach its embrace, we are coming toward something that I believe is sacred; something that holds mystery and power.

I think that it's fitting that this is the way it should be. We shouldn't need to expect that the labyrinth should give up its secrets easily. All we need to do is walk and–if we can–to give up a little of our trust in our own ego's version of 'truth' for just a short while.

The Alpha and the Omega

For me, the labyrinth represents what might be called the 'Alpha and Omega' of a person's life and its integration into the 'whole' – the merging of an individual with one, single essence. This is certainly my perception when arriving at the center, and noticing that I'm just but one part of the ever changing constellation of walkers around me.

If the 'Alpha' is the egotistical individual (much in the way the 'Alpha male' describes someone who's driven to dominate in a group), then the 'Omega' is the whole, the true Self, and the transcending of the individual.

The center is a place of integration: a place to rest awhile and be absorbed by what is happening all around. Appropriately, perhaps, the Greek letter Omega translates into English as 'the big O' – and this is one way I like to describe the space that the labyrinth contains. That said, my view is biased by my interest in mysticism and spirituality. It is just one possible explanation for the labyrinth's power.

Experiences along the path

What then happens when you step into a labyrinth?

Simply put: there is no one common experience that accompanies every walk. Many varied experiences may be encountered by different people at different times, as well as by the same person on different walks. Every walk happens for the first time. Every walk is unique.

Let me try to describe an example of one of my own walks, although I must be careful to stress that I'm not sure that this might be described as 'typical'. Everyone's walk is unique, after all! For the purpose of my illustration, I refer to a walk that's hosted by a facilitator, rather than walking a labyrinth that's freely accessible at any time.

I usually approach the labyrinth with a view to letting go of the myriad busy thoughts that are running through my mind – seeing it as a place to meditate, and to accept whatever may come to me through images, thoughts, or feelings. In other words, my normal path toward the center isn't premeditated by a specific question or expectation of what I might experience. I simply let myself 'go', seeing that this may be the only chance that I have during the day to do so.

Where the opportunity exists, I typically wait awhile after the labyrinth has been opened, until it feels right for me to step forward to begin my walk. Nothing more than a gentle impulse may be involved in prompting me to make this move, but the nudge usually seems to come from somewhere inside of me, rather than being deliberately thought through...I'm not usually making a calculation like 'now I can see there is a large gap opening up between the walkers ahead of me, therefore now is my moment to make my move!'

Of course, one or several other people might feel the urge to approach the labyrinth at the same time as me. In such case, I will take my turn in the queue, until the host of the walk ushers me to step onto the path. However, I like to wait a moment just outside the labyrinth's entrance point before taking my first step. This gives me a chance to acknowledge that I'm stepping into a different space than the one that I'm coming from – a mark of respect for the labyrinth, much in the same way that (say) a devotee of the Roman Catholic Church might make the sign of the cross with their hand when approaching a church altar.

I believe that when we take our first step into the labyrinth, we are crossing a threshold. Whether or not this is to step into a liminal space (a place where we have left what is familiar to us behind, but don't yet know what we might find in a new situation we are coming toward), I do not know, but for me, to step into a labyrinth is to leave the outside world behind me.

The concept of crossing a threshold is itself one further purpose to which the labyrinth has been put. As a ritual in ceremony, stepping over a line, or through or under some physical construction representing a boundary, often symbolizes a commitment to move into a new stage of life.

In a rite of passage ceremony–for example, where a young woman or man passes from childhood into adulthood–to face such a boundary and then step over to the other side indicates that person's readiness to take on the new responsibilities that will face them in their new chapter of life. The initiation of adolescents into adulthood in some tribes in Africa, for example, codifies this rite of transition into a labyrinthine dance (such as the Domba Dance, performed by young women of the Venda people).

Consequently, the labyrinth can serve a powerful role in ceremonies that mark important life transitions.

Stepping onto a labyrinth isn't normally associated with moving from one phase of life to another, but I do believe every walk involves acknowledging the possibility that you will be changed in some way, even if this may not immediately be apparent.

I walk at whatever pace seems right. The movement along the path isn't a race, and perhaps sometimes, as Gernot Candolini observes, "Those who travel along too quickly often hurry past the center without noticing it" [13].

I maintain 'soft eyes', or a gaze that isn't too firmly fixed on anything in particular. I'm normally dimly aware in my peripheral vision of the paths that others around me might be taking, and I notice where I'm placing my feet, but otherwise my focus is generally inside myself. I'm not even thinking about arriv-

Labyrinth A-Ω

ing at the center, and it doesn't matter if I do (the journey is what matters, not reaching a destination).

My pace may quicken at times, and slow down at others. Sometimes, I may feel that I just want to rest awhile, focusing on the passage of breath through my body, or becoming aware of my feet's strong connection with the ground (much like a sense of the tree having its roots firmly planted in the earth below).

Some labyrinth designs, such is the Chartres design, offer points where it's possible to step off the path of the labyrinth for a short while. These features, such as the double-bitted axe shape seen in the Chartres pattern, are spaces where it's possible to stand, sit or kneel for a while, without interrupting the passage of other walkers.

However, passing alongside or in front of another person, or being passed by another, is another aspect of the labyrinth's beauty. Of course, it's possible to walk a labyrinth alone, but when others share the space with you, more often than not, this creates special moments of awareness that we are each a part of a greater whole. There's something quite special about the energy of walking a labyrinth in common with others.

It's often said that the labyrinth is a metaphor for life – that people are following their own life paths, but that we are all moving toward the same destination (to realize our full potential as individuals, to be saved from the tribulations of everyday life, or to find enlightenment). During life's journey, of course, we encounter others – sometimes coming toward us, sometimes passing us by, and at other times just featuring on the periphery of our attention. Such encounters happen in the labyrinth too, but without involving an exchange of words or—at worse—a crossing of swords.

We don't know what others may be experiencing during their walks, what thoughts may preoccupy them – all we are aware of is that we are each going forward, at our own pace and in our own way.

If the labyrinth models life in the everyday, then it can also be thought of as representing the full cycle of life – from birth at the entrance way, through to 'dying' to old ways of thinking and behaving at the center, and then emerging from the labyrinth as though reborn.

This might be considered to be an exclusively Christian way of thinking about one aspect of the labyrinth's symbolism. However, the notion of life as a cycle of death and rebirth is well rooted in Eastern traditions as well as in pagan thinking too; for example in the Hindu, Buddhist, and Druid traditions (for Druids, a circular space also represents the cycle of the seasons, with its outer rim representing the orbit of the earth and its center symbolizing the sun, the source of all life on Earth).

I've most often become aware of others when I'm walking the outer circuit of the labyrinth. My observation is that I tend to be the person who moves around the edges of life quite a lot, often feeling content in my solitude, but taking comfort from the fact that I'm not really alone.

Labyrinth A-Ω

My walking pace often picks up on the outer circuit too – I don't know why this may be so, but this seems to have something to do with gathering a momentum toward the center, often with a 'clear road' ahead of me. Life itself, of course, involves periods when we seem to move forward at quite a pace, as well as those when we feel slowed down. Small observations of this kind that might accompany a walk are examples of the sort of reflections that come to the surface that might otherwise normally pass us by.

There's something too about moving in a circular direction that generates a flow of energy. Charles Darwin famously used to walk a circuitous sand walk in his Garden in Kent, where it's said that he formed his theories about the origin of species. This practice appears to have been very beneficial in helping him form his views.

In a similar vein, one modern application of the labyrinth is for problem solving. For example, Sig Lonegren describes a technique in which a separate question relating to a problem can be pondered on each circuit of a classical labyrinth [14].

Spirals can have a similar affect, although strictly speaking, a spiral isn't a labyrinth. The former brings someone who walks it continuously closer to the center and may not be virtually entirely enclosed by an outer perimeter. The path of a labyrinth, by contrast, usually approximates to orbits of different size, or has a 'coming and going' route toward the center.

We should note that labyrinths aren't always circular in form, neither are their paths always smoothly sinuous. The installations at the cathedrals in Amiens, France, and Ely, UK, for example, display a very angular pattern. Nevertheless, a well-defined perimeter contains these and all labyrinths, and it will be apparent to any walker who walks them that they are moving around and ultimately toward a center.

Many labyrinth designs, such as the familiar pattern seen in the medieval style, involve frequent turns that take us back in the direction from which we've just come. An ingenious feature of the medieval (Chartres) pattern is that its sinuous path at times comes close to the center, and then takes a walker away toward the outer edge again. Unless you are very familiar with this pattern and consciously noting the course of your walk, it's difficult to know where you are along the path – the center may be very close, or yet still some distance away.

I find that the coming and going, toward and away from the center, often causes me to 'wake up' at turns if I find that my mind is wandering onto everyday things – serving as a reminder to 'switch off' and just allow myself to walk.

There's something about moving the whole body in this 'coming and going' pattern that is very energizing, and I sense that the playing out of energies is amplified by the relationship of our changing position relative to others who are progressing along their own walks. Physicists might step in to offer an analogy with the gravitational pull of the stars and planets, but I will let such comparisons pass without questioning their significance.

For pilgrims who had made long journeys to come to the cathedral at Chartres and elsewhere, coming to the labyrinth's center must have felt like finally arriving at the gateway to Heaven itself. For me, arriving at the heart is normally just a point on the journey. I usually feel inclined to wait here awhile, often sitting down and closing my eyes, feeling secure and grounded, allowing the quiet movement of fellow walkers around me to merge into a blur.

However, for many, arriving in the center has greater significance. This is, as Virgina Westbury puts it, "[a place that symbolizes] wholeness and completion, the heart of the matter, our human heart" [15].

On the occasions when I've taken a question with me into the labyrinth, a rest at the center offers an opportunity to hear and receive whatever may come – or to wait a little while for a possible response, if I'm unsure that I've received anything (in fact, what is received may be perceived at a subconscious level). My outward path is then one of being grateful for what I've received, and of being open to how I might integrate this into my everyday life.

As with resting before starting my walk, I often wait for some small inner prompting to journey back from the center. While still contained within the space of the labyrinth, my outward journey often seems to move at a quicker pace than my inward one. I'm conscious that I am, step-by-step, moving closer to the point where I will again need to cross the threshold back into the everyday world, leaving the sanctuary of the labyrinth behind. This may not be a prospect that I always welcome, but I'm conscious that it's usually the case that I will step off the labyrinth better prepared to face the day ahead of me than before I stepped onto it. I am returning in some way transformed, even–at least, metaphorically speaking–reborn.

If the labyrinth is sometimes likened to the great womb of nature, as is thought to be understood by the creators of the early Baltic labyrinths, then there might be some truth in the notion that the labyrinth is a place for rebirthing – or where we might be prepared to emerge back into the world having being transformed.

Some have argued that something similar happens when we are in deep sleep – that we connect with a level of consciousness that allows us to reflect upon, learn from, and equips us to respond to the challenges that may lay ahead of us. Through such close encounters with our inner selves, the soul might grow.

Again, we are in the territory of conjecture here, but I suspect that something more powerful than we might realize happens when we make our move toward the heart of the labyrinth. I agree with Sig Lonegren, who asserts that "labyrinths can work real magic – moments that bring worlds together...enhancing the possibility of bringing together our analytical or rational mode of consciousness with our intuitive or spiritual levels of consciousness" [16].

Certainly, it's the case for me that I find my breathing rate calming and tension being released from my body. And were I wearing an EEG headset during my walk, more than likely, I would learn that my brainwaves are following the pattern of Alpha or Theta rather than Beta waves – the types that aid calmness, and help integrate the mind and body. This would fit with the pattern observed in studies of individuals in deep meditation, as well as those who have come into a period of deep sleep [17].

I usually hesitate a little before stepping out of the labyrinth; but only briefly, because I know that my walk must end. As when crossing the labyrinth's threshold when I begin my walk, once stepping outside its space, I usually turn to silently offer thanks for what it has given me, before returning to my seat.

What I have described is but one example of a walk. Every walk that I've taken in the labyrinth has been different, presenting unexpected thoughts, images, and feelings. Most of all, each walk has touched me in some way – I've felt at peace, secure, and sometimes, disturbed. The changes that may occur in the labyrinth are ones that I trust to be helpful to me, and relevant for the point that I have reached in my life. I'm sure that the same will be true for every other person, even though their experiences may be very different from my own.

Enough for now about what happens for an individual in the labyrinth. I'd like to return now to consider some of the many applications for labyrinth walking that we haven't yet touched upon.

Applications of the labyrinth

One good example to start with is a labyrinth that's been used with the purpose of reconciling differences after a period of conflict. The Reconciliation Labyrinth in South Africa incorporates two entrances into its design. Clare Wilson, its designer, explains that the two portals represent the different starting places that South Africans have arrived from following the years of apartheid.

At the same time, this unusual design serves as a reminder that, while the experiences that have led individuals to where they come from may be very different, in stepping forward, each walker does so with a common desire to heal the wounds of division and, as Wilson puts it, "to grow in the strength of our diversity, to make a start on our journeys toward... [creating a] South Africa where people really care about each other and what life's experiences have done to us" [18].

By passing beside others, and walking the same path that they have trodden, the labyrinth helps individuals to appreciate how their own lives have been

Labyrinth A-Ω

shaped, before they arrive at a common, shared center.

The first labyrinth incorporating the reconciliation pattern was inaugurated in a suburb of Cape Town in 2002. Many more have since been established across the country, either on a permanent or temporary basis. One now stands as a permanent fixture alongside Slangkop Lighthouse in Kommetje, not far from Cape Town. Here, three day education courses are taught for children, each of whom is offered a chance to walk the labyrinth alongside their fellow young citizens in the making, who often come from differing backgrounds and neighborhoods.

Wilson's design has been replicated elsewhere in the world – including in schools, therapeutic, and community settings. The labyrinth's role in building bridges often plays out on an individual-to-individual or organization-to-organization basis, as much as in providing a way forward following a strained period in a nation's history. For example, one such labyrinth in California is being used to assist divorced parents to find ways of working together, especially to resolve to respect the common ground that's needed for protecting their children's interests [19].

The potential for labyrinths to serve a unifying and peacemaking purpose is exemplified in other initiatives too. At the 2002 Salt Lake City Winter Olympics, for example, a 7-circuit labyrinth was inaugurated as one means for encouraging a coming together of staff, athletes, and visitors from different nations.

This 'World Peace Labyrinth' incorporated seven globes in its design, symbolizing the seven continents. By coming to the labyrinth, walkers were able to share in a common, nondenominational, and peaceful practice.

Taking inspiration from the Salt Lake City example, Florida-based Presbyterian Church minister and labyrinth facilitator Kathryn McLean co-created a portable version in the same design, which she has used for numerous community-building initiatives across her home state and elsewhere.

Other labyrinth initiatives have been intended to aid healing and community restoration among communities that are recovering from a collective trauma. Examples include labyrinths at Long Beach, Mississippi, which was used to help local communities to rebuild their lives following the devastation of Hurricane Katrina, as well as following oil spills in the Gulf; a labyrinth at Trinity Wall Street/St Paul's Church close to Ground Zero in New York City; and a labyrinth used by servicemen in the 30th AG Battalion, offering a quiet haven for reflection and reintegration following their return from service in Iraq or Afghanistan.

The value of labyrinths for community building has been recognized by many neighborhood and city authorities. Labyrinths have been commissioned to be installed in public parks, city squares, and other public spaces, often exciting the imagination and galvanizing the participation of individuals in their creation.

Labyrinth A-Ω

For example, in the tower square in the mountain settlement of La Falda in Argentina—a town to which many Nazis fled following the end of World War II—one such labyrinth has been co-created by townsfolk with the support of their municipality, along with the help of a team from the leading California-based labyrinth organization, Veriditas.

"We hope that our labyrinth will be useful in helping people come together, reconciling old hatreds, bringing healing," comments Judith Tripp, one of the fourteen labyrinth advocates who traveled to La Falda to assist in the labyrinth's design and foundation work [20].

An equally valuable legacy that has helped popularize labyrinth walking in another part of the world is the impressive sandstone installation at Centennial Park in Sydney, Australia. This permanent fixture is modeled on the Chartres design, and largely came into being as a result of the vision and dedication of just one woman.

The project began as the idea of Emily Simpson, who had been inspired to bring a labyrinth to her home city following her discovery of the labyrinth's unifying power during a tour of Scotland. Following years of hard work and fundraising, the Sydney Centennial Park Labyrinth was dedicated in 2014 in front of representatives from the city's many different faith traditions, alongside supporters who had helped Emily raise the A$500,000 needed to bring the project to fruition.

One of the wisdom keepers of the Sydney project, Aboriginal elder of the Biripi Nation, Aunty Ali Golding, summed up what this particular labyrinth has come to mean for many people:

"Walking home to country is a connection our people have always had with Mother Earth. Our culture is defined by the closeness of family circles and staying connected to the people within it. The labyrinth invites and welcomes people to walk the path together – it calls them to the land in oneness."

Several years on from its inauguration, regularly walking the labyrinth has become an important part of the lives of many Sydneysiders. Sunset group walks are often held there, and every day, busy commuters, mothers with pushchairs, and visitors from far afield, stop by to pause in the labyrinth's calm space.

Community involvement in labyrinth construction is evidenced in projects around the world. As with the La Falda initiative, individuals from different localities and cultures have come together to share in this task.

The charismatic Houston-based artist Reginald Adams is among those who have inspired and led such projects, including a labyrinth that brought high school and college students from Texas together with teenagers in Ecuador to co-create a labyrinth by the Equator, close to Quito. Reginald has lent his talents to labyrinth projects in inner-city areas too, including one built on the rubble of a torn-down church in his home city, that continues to provide a space where former churchgoers and their neighbors can come together to contemplate, have fellowship, and pray.

The community-building focus has been taken on in organizational settings too – including labyrinths that have appeared in university campuses, hospitals, and in the grounds of corporate headquarters.

At the Myanmar Institute of Theology, for example, a labyrinth was created by faculty, staff, and students, with the express purpose of fostering the spiritual life of the community. The labyrinth was laid out with a prayer that those who walked it would find a connection with God. Within a short time of it being completed, individuals began reporting incidents of healing as a result of walking the labyrinth's path. One man who had been suffering irregular heartbeats reported that his heartbeat had returned to normal after his encounter with the labyrinth; a woman reported feeling 'lifted up' when she walked, despite having a weak heart and doubting that she had the physical capacity to walk the path [21].

An increasing body of evidence supports the healing qualities of labyrinth walking. In an examination of published research, Dr Herbert Benson of Harvard Medical School's Mind/Body Institute is convinced that such practice leads to both reduced blood pressure and improved respiration rates [22]. Chronic pain, anxiety, and insomnia, are among other conditions that available evidence strongly suggests are reduced through regular walking of a labyrinth, quite apart from the obvious relaxation benefits.

Jeff Saward, a leading authority in labyrinth research, suggests ways in which we may respond to the labyrinth: "The labyrinth can be a pathway of prayer, an opportunity to connect with the Divine and contemplate the magic and mystery of existence...[its] charms invite playfulness as well as soulfulness, delight and curiosity as well as contemplation" [23].

In a similar vein, an extensive review by John W. Rhodes of 16 studies that had explored the positive affects of engaging with a labyrinth [24] adds weight to the suggestion that labyrinth walking offers many potential benefits.

Rhodes distinguishes between physical responses to interacting with the labyrinth (such things as increased calm, reduced stress and anxiety), and 'state of mind' affects that appear to emerge from these (such as heightened clarity, greater openness, and reflectiveness). It's these 'states of mind', Rhodes suggests, that might make a walker more receptive to flashes of inspiration, hunches, and the like.

In her study of the affects of the labyrinth's use at the Myanmar Institute of Theology, Jill Geoffrion takes an alternative perspective, distinguishing between several types of healing that are reported by walkers – including emotional, spiritual, relational, and social healing. "The labyrinth appears to be a safe place in which people feel free to explore their deep fears as well as their desires related to the communities in which they live," Geoffrion observes. "[There are] many ways in which praying in the labyrinth has resulted in a greater sense of wholeness and health" [25].

Some of the comments offered by walkers of the labyrinth at the Myanmar Institute of Theology and elsewhere certainly seem to bear this out:

"This was the first time my mind had been free of distractions in the past three years."'

"While praying [in] the labyrinth, I was released from stress bondage."

"I was very moved by the experience and found a sense of peace."

"Since walking the labyrinth over a period of time, the depression that had settled over me when my husband died has lifted."

Appropriately then, labyrinths have found their way into hospitals, hospices, and care homes. The labyrinth at the Pilgrims Hospice in Canterbury, UK, is one of many centers where a labyrinth now plays an important part in the palliative care of those coping with life-threatening illness.

In other therapeutic settings, individuals have reported similar experiences, including what have occasionally been life changing ones. This has been the case at such centers as Cottonwood Tucson, Arizona, a residential center dedicated to the treatment of substance abuse, mood disorders, and unresolved trauma. Many patients who have walked the labyrinth there affirm that their encounter helped them confront deeply rooted issues, such as feeling ready to address areas that arouse great fear for them and from which they had been running away [26].

It seems clear that the affects of labyrinth walking can be very profound. But for many, the opportunity to escape the busyness of the everyday, to reconnect with oneself, or simply to be uninterrupted for a short while are sufficient reasons for returning to the labyrinth time and time again.

Labyrinths may have many diverse applications, but ultimately, they demand nothing more from us than we simply step into their embrace, walk, and be. As the Venerable Boan Sunim, of Korean Puri Temple, Gordon, Sydney so aptly puts it, "Look at your feet. There is your mind. See where your feet are. You are there" [27].

CHAPTER 3

How to Approach the Labyrinth?

AS WE'VE SEEN, labyrinths have been used for many different purposes, as well as for many more other than those that we've discussed. But how should one approach the labyrinth as an individual, or indeed, as a community of individuals?

Earlier, I described aspects of my experience during a labyrinth walk. As I mentioned, this was to illustrate an example of what might happen when stepping into the labyrinth's space. It isn't by any means what you may discover through your own experience.

In fact, every time we step into the labyrinth, we should expect to have a new experience. This is a little like life itself – every time we embark on something new, we can't fully anticipate what may happen.

In my own practice, I don't normally take a question with me into the labyrinth. But this isn't always the case. In fact, when I have had a particularly important question that I'm seeking guidance for, I will approach the labyrinth with the very purpose of holding open my question during my inward walk, opening myself to receive whatever answer may come. Some labyrinth hosts may offer cards containing a word, phrase, or thought, that may be left by the entrance to the labyrinth for those who may wish to take one with them during their walk as a possible focus for reflection.

A response to a question posed may not come immediately, but often an idea, a word from my inner voice, or a feeling does come. What's more, to temporarily lose sight of a question that we might consciously have brought with us into the labyrinth doesn't mean that that question doesn't still have relevance – when we ask with real intention, our subconscious is perfectly capable of holding open our enquiry, as well as being acutely sensitive to receiving answers.

At other times, I may aim to keep my focus on how I'm taking each step as I move forward. Here, the invitation is to pay attention to how our feet make contact with the ground as we take each step – being conscious of how we flex each leg as we take one step forward, then bringing the heel of the forward foot into contact with the ground, before arching the whole sole of the foot, and finally making full contact with the earth below.

Labyrinth A-Ω

Still at other times, I may wish to recite a mantra–a single word or simple phrase–as a means for anchoring my attention as I follow the labyrinth's path. One simple mantra that I occasionally like to repeat takes the words of the renowned Zen Master, Thich Nhat Hanh [28]:

"Breathing in, I calm my body and mind. Breathing out, I smile –

Dwelling in the present moment, I know this is the only moment."

For me, this is a wonderfully powerful way of keeping in touch with the present, as each phrase is recited as I take a breath. 'Breathing in, calm... Breathing out, smile...'

Even when using an 'anchor', such as a mantra or a focus on a question, it's not uncommon to lose sight of this as your meditation deepens during the course of a walk. And when your busy mind stops calling for attention, this is generally an indication that you've managed to let go of your ego mind for a time, and have become more aware of the usually gentle counseling of your inner voice.

Being sensitive to what ideas or suggestions may come to you in such moments can be especially edifying, because these (often) fleeting moments are ones when we come close to being in touch with our true selves.

All this may sound very mystical and beyond the ken of someone who just wants to try a labyrinth walk. However, there's no need to worry about what you may or may not experience when taking your first steps into the labyrinth. I mention the possibility for coming into quite a deep meditative state simply because this isn't an uncommon experience.

The truth is that there are no set experiences that come from being open to the labyrinth's embrace. As we've said before, every walk is unique. There is no right or wrong – what will be will be.

The same 'no one way' principle applies to how you physically move from a labyrinth's entrance to its center, and back again. The host of a walk may typically suggest some guidelines to follow, both before and after walking, and when moving around the labyrinth itself. These may include such things as respecting the space and silence of others (if non-verbal acknowledgement happens when you pass by another person, that may be fine; but normally, fellow walkers will be alone in their reflection).

Practical matters that are intended to help preserve the life of the labyrinth may also be mentioned, such as an invitation to remove muddy boots, for example, and mentioning how the walk will be brought to an end (for example, by the chiming of a bell, or by becoming aware of when the host begins

Labyrinth A-Ω

to slowly circle around the perimeter of the labyrinth's space).

Generally, such ground rules are designed to ensure that everyone who shares a walk respects each other, as well as respecting the labyrinth itself, and to tie in with everyday logistical concerns that need to be observed, such as the time available for the walk.

Such guidance excepted, there really are no rules for what you do once you step over the labyrinth's threshold. Hold your arms out, bring them into the form of a diagonal cross across your body (this is not an exclusively symbolic gesture for Christians, but it is also a self comforting way for maintaining good posture), or let them hang by your side.

Walk at whichever pace seems right – slowing down and speeding up as you feel inclined, occasionally making a stop, sensing whatever feels right in the moment. Others may step around you when their pace is moving them forward more quickly than your own, and of course, you may at times feel the need to pass by others who are ahead of you on the path.

At the center–if you reach there–you may wish to wait awhile, or you may prefer to embark on your outward walk without pausing. Some labyrinth designs may involve taking a different path away from the center than the one from which you approached; others will invite you to return along the same path.

There is of course no need to reach the center, perhaps because this doesn't feel right, or alternatively because the time available for the walk is limited. Simply turn around at a point, and then return along the same path that brought you to where you are now.

When you finish your walk, you may want to wait awhile before leaving to carry on with your day. Continue to be respectful to those who are still walking, for those who may not yet have started their walk, and to those who are reflecting on the experiences that the labyrinth has brought them.

A host may suggest that it's acceptable to leave quietly when you feel ready, or they may invite you to remain until everyone has completed their walks.

Facilitated walks may also involve some variation on how the session is conducted. For example, at the church where I first began regularly walking, while our numbers were still small, I and fellow walkers used to gather at the center to listen to a brief reading before continuing our journeys out again. I used to value these moments of being in a small circle with my friends, each of us having followed the path that brought us there in our own way, but now having arrived at a common center. These walks were also prefaced by a brief reading, which was offered as a possible theme for reflection during the inward walk.

Of course, not all labyrinths are hosted by a facilitator. In public places where a labyrinth is permanently or often accessible, there are normally few constraints in terms of the time that you may wish to take for your walk.

Walking a labyrinth is often described as being a 'metaphor for life', in that we don't know who we might meet along our path, nor what experiences we might enjoy

You may at times be alone, and at others be joined by a group. If you do find yourself walking a labyrinth alone, I suggest following the same principles that are usually offered as guidance by the host of a facilitated walk – respecting the silence and, if you will, 'sacredness' of the space, and respecting the labyrinth itself. This probably means that if you're a skater or skateboarder, setting aside your rollerblades for a short while might be a good idea. And if you're an obsessive Tweeter or texter, putting your phone on silence may help you pay better attention to the matter in hand!

I hope that the preceding preamble will convince you that there's nothing to fear in approaching the labyrinth: no concerns about 'doing the wrong thing', or standing out as an ignorant newcomer who will surely fail to take some essential step that's known only to experienced labyrinth walkers. Happily, the labyrinth makes no distinction between novices and those who've entered its space perhaps a thousand times before.

The same may be said of groups who want to begin a regular labyrinth practice. The group that I joined began as a small gathering of just two or three. A regular time for meeting was scheduled into our diaries, volunteers were identified to help lay out and later pack away the newly purchased canvas, and our one trained labyrinth facilitator stepped forward as our regular host. Innovations such as starting each walk with a brief reading, gathering together at the center, and making available cards with suggestions for reflection for those who wanted them, came later through mutual discussion.

If you're considering bringing a labyrinth into your organization, club, or community, I suggest that it will be valuable to engage the help of an experienced facilitator for a while, if you're able. Alternatively, you may wish to investigate the possibility of one member of your group becoming trained as a facilitator. Training is invaluable, drawing as it does on the thousands of hours' of collective experience of labyrinth hosts, and minimizing the risk that inappropriate facilitation might lead to newcomers to the labyrinth having a bad first experience. Veriditas offers a long-established training program for facilitators (contact details are at the back of this book).

Labyrinth A-Ω

Committing to purchase a Labyrinth, or to have one permanently installed, can involve a large investment initially. Options are available for avoiding high start-up costs, such as loaning a labyrinth or creating a 'pop-up' version. We'll consider several possible options of this kind in the following chapter.

If funds are available for commissioning a labyrinth, it may be acceptable to invite small contributions from those who benefit from walking the labyrinth over time – although ideally on a voluntary basis, and recognizing individuals' differing abilities and willingness to pay.

My own sense is that labyrinth initiatives that aim to encourage a coming together of people, such as for fostering strong neighbor and community relationships, can be enhanced if all members of the group feel they have a part to play in determining how the venture evolves.

Offering a brief opportunity for those who are able to share their reflections following a walk, combined with a chance for getting to know others by sharing in general conversation, is one effective means for inviting participation. Such activity encourages an enhanced social purpose for a group's meetings at the same time.

As with any group that aims to be inclusive, it's important to ensure that newcomers feel welcome. This is where a host can play an especially important role – offering a simple introduction and words of guidance when noticing a new face. Verbal introductions might be backed up by a simple handout, offered to newcomers to help make them feel at ease and to appreciate how the group's labyrinth practice normally works out. An example handout can be downloaded from the Labyrinth Around America website (www.labyrintharoundamerica.net).

One further consideration when having a temporary labyrinth made or a permanent one installed, is to take time to decide what design seems right for the group's normal use. The medieval (for example, Chartres), classical, and Baltic types are most common, but there's no restriction on creating a design of your own.

Important considerations for the design might include whether it's intended that the labyrinth be used for more than one purpose (for example, playing a part in occasional ceremonies as well as offering 'open space' opportunities for regular walkers), and assessing the relative benefits of choosing a so-called 'processional' labyrinth over one that involves walkers returning along the same path (a procession meaning that a separate exit pathway is provided to that used to reach the center from the entranceway).

Other considerations will include the size of labyrinth that can be accommodated relative to the space available, the width and length of the labyrinth's path (for example, to take account of the needs of wheelchair users), and the material used for creating the labyrinth.

The colors used for delimiting the labyrinth's path may also need to be thought through – different colors have different energies that may or may not feel appropriate, and practical considerations, such as the ability to see the contrast between the painted lines and the path itself, may come into play in your decision making.

When installing a permanent labyrinth, an experienced labyrinth designer and builder should normally be consulted as a part of the process. Experienced constructors will be able to advise on aspects of the installation that might not otherwise be appreciated, such as the appropriate siting of the labyrinth, and considerations relating to the underlying ground structure and drainage (in the case of outdoor projects). For those with an interest in the geomantic significance for a siting, an experienced geomancer might also be consulted.

Nevertheless, many communities have established labyrinths under their own steam, taking advantage of the various excellent printed and online materials that offer guidance in labyrinth construction and design (a list of suppliers is provided at the end of this book).

I firmly believe that if there is a will among a small number of individuals or a larger community to bring a labyrinth project to fruition, then the group will find its way to make this happen. Very much like there being no hard and fast rules for walking a labyrinth, every community project is unique. Every initiative is special, and the labyrinth will always reward those who take time to nurture their vision.

Clive Johnson

CHAPTER 4

Where Next for your Labyrinth Journey?

AFTER FIRST ENCOUNTERING the labyrinth, most people find it captivating. However, a labyrinth walked in a distant place or as part of a traveling roadshow may be inspiring as a single event, but for those who want to tread its path again, what options are available?

Finding a labyrinth

It may be that you're fortune enough to have a labyrinth in your neighborhood – one that's permanently available in a park or city square, for example, or a portable version that's regularly laid out in a church, garden, or community hall. A simple Internet search should be sufficient to identify whether any such labyrinths exist nearby.

One excellent online resource that's specifically designed to help connect labyrinths with people that want to walk them is The Labyrinth Locator (www.labyrinthlocator.com). This extensive resource, sponsored by The Labyrinth Society and Veriditas, provides a searchable directory of hundreds of labyrinths worldwide. With just a few simple clicks, the website will list any labyrinths that can be found in a particular locality.

Other resources for locating labyrinths are available too, with several being listed at the back of this book.

Making or buying a labyrinth

Of course, you may prefer to set about creating a labyrinth of your own, whether for a group or for your own personal use. Examples abound of labyrinths that have been formed with paving stones in backyards, cut into lawns, or painted onto playgrounds.

Baltic, medieval, and classical labyrinth patterns can be drawn relatively easily with the aid of some basic knowledge and a few basic tools (such as a square rule, tape measure, and a length of string). Their outline can be quickly replicated by working from what is known as a 'seed pattern', a simple blueprint of lines and marker points that's mapped out close to the labyrinth's center. The diagram be-

Labyrinth A-Ω

low illustrates the process for drawing a classical style labyrinth, building up from such a pattern.

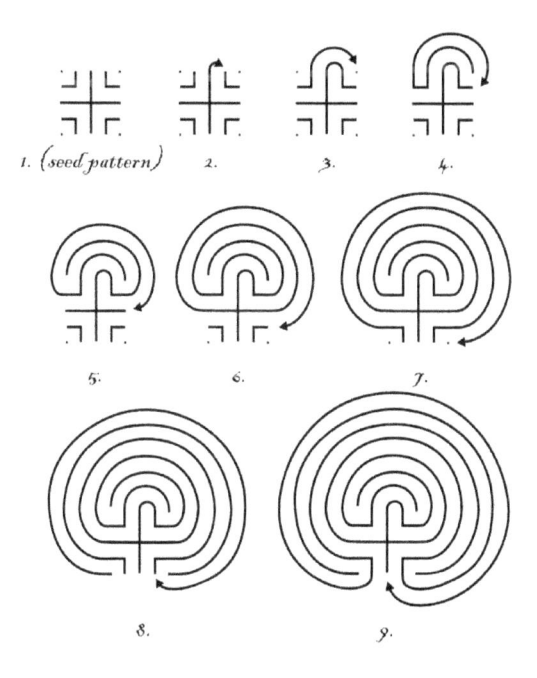

1. (seed pattern) 2. 3. 4.

5. 6. 7.

8. 9.

Method for drawing a classical labyrinth

A range of YouTube videos, books, and other materials describe how to mark out different labyrinth designs. A host of examples are listed at the back of this book.

'Pop-up' labyrinths—ones that are intended to be set up and then dismantled after a single event—may be created using a wide range of inexpensive materials. Bungee rope, masking tape, candles, and chalk lines are among possibilities for marking out a temporary path. A labyrinth that's cut into a beach, snow, or the soil of an uncultivated field need not cost anything at all to make, even if it may not be very long lasting.

Polycanvas and acrylic are especially popular as base materials for portable labyrinths, offering both durability and weatherproofing. Other materials may lend themselves for more regular outdoor use, for example, UPS fabric, the type of material that's often used to produce temporary advertising banners.

However, virtually any material will suffice for creating an indoor labyrinth that will have relatively limited use, especially if walkers take care to respect the damageable nature of the material that they are walking on (for example, by removing footwear before stepping on to it).

If you don't wish to experiment with creating a portable labyrinth of your own, help can be obtained from a number of well established labyrinth makers (a number of whom are listed at the back of this book). Many of these can also assist with creating artwork for designs other than the more common patterns. For example, the work of Lisa Moriarty, the creator of the labyrinth for Labyrinth Around America, includes examples of labyrinths that incorporate a tree illusion branch motif, are focused around a heart-shaped center, and ones that echo the angular shape of many labyrinths that are seen in Roman mosaics, among others. The portfolios of other suppliers are similarly varied.

Projects to introduce labyrinths in a public space, as well as in such places as university grounds, corporate campuses, and rest homes, may call for a more permanent installation. Such projects typically require larger budgets, and will be greatly assisted by drawing on the expertise of a specialist labyrinth builder.

Even here, costs can often be minimized where volunteers are ready to become involved in the project. For example, a labor of love combined with construction expertise, helped create the beautiful 'Tree of Life' labyrinth that is sheltered by two giant oak trees in the grounds of Grace Episcopal Church in Houston, Texas.

Lap-top labyrinths and labyrinths for the home

All this may be well and good for individuals who have the money, time, and reason to make or commission a labyrinth to be made for them, not to mention having the space for laying out their new creation.

However, most of us don't enjoy such luxuries, and some may not have easy access to a public labyrinth close to their homes. Fortunately, options exist for folks who find themselves in this situation.

'Walking' a finger labyrinth is one possibility for individuals who are short of space or who are physically unable to walk a traditional labyrinth. In this labyrinth, the path is a groove, typically carved into wood, molded in ceramic, or crafted using some other material, and the means for locomotion is by moving a finger, as opposed to the feet and legs.

Finger labyrinths of different sizes and weights are available from online stores and elsewhere. Most are designed to sit in the lap or to rest on a small side table. Their slim form makes them easy to store, although they may also serve as an attractive table decoration.

Finger labyrinths also have an important role to play in allowing people who might not otherwise be able to walk a ground labyrinth to share in this precious experience, including those who are bed-bound or blind. Neal Harris, a professional counselor, finger labyrinth creator, and a founding member of The Labyrinth Society, has used hand labyrinths in various therapeutic settings for more than twenty years.

Harris' work led him to pioneer a double labyrinth, involving the use of both hands (or being used by two people), which helps to balance the activity of the right and left hemispheres of the brain. 'Walking' such a labyrinth has helped stroke patients who have suffered brain damage to heal, among others [29].

Finger labyrinths have what I believe is an advantage over their larger cousins – offering a walker the ability to close their eyes while they are walking if they wish, which for many people can be an aid for avoiding distraction during their meditation.

A labyrinth that can be traced using a finger need not be carved in wood or stone. A path drawn on a sheet of paper can serve the same purpose, not to mention one embroidered onto a cushion cover or rug, projected onto a wall (or even a swimming pool, in the case of a special event staged at Nottingham University), or temporarily marked out in a sandbox.

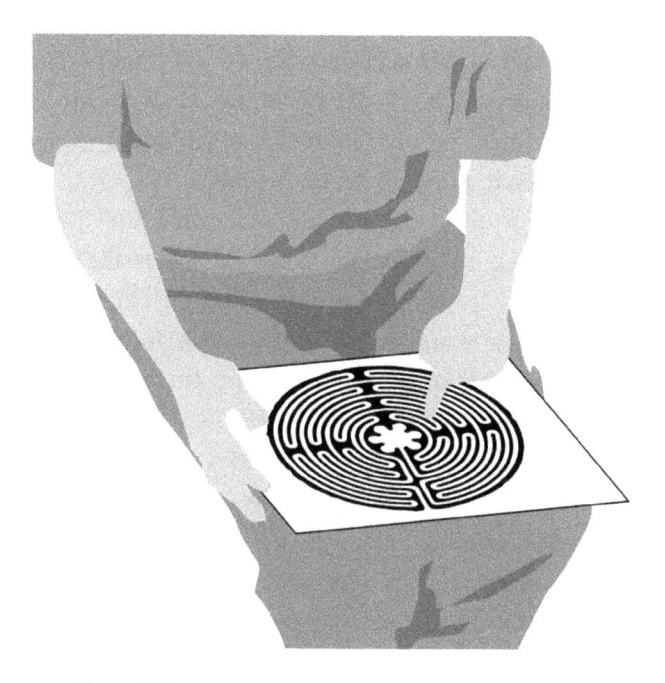

A finger labyrinth requires very little room to store and can be used by the home-bound

Labyrinths have been crafted into pottery, knitted into blanket squares, and carved with a finger out of play dough. Lisa Moriarty's portfolio even includes a labyrinth that was cut into a pumpkin – perhaps a special creation for Halloween! There really is virtually no limitation to what might be used for creating a labyrinth.

A labyrinth that's depicted on a poster, or that's projected onto a wall can be 'walked' not only by tracing it's path with a finger, but by following its course with the eyes. Such an approach may offer a means of connecting with the labyrinth's path for someone who is paralyzed, not to mention anyone who may be able to find a small space of wall on which to pin a labyrinth drawing.

For all of us, walking a labyrinth isn't just about moving a part of our body, but is, as Paula D'Arcy puts it, "[a walk] not only with feet, but with hands, and hearts and minds" [30]. A walk for the heart and mind–the most important of these–need involve very little physical movement.

With so many opportunities available for engaging with the labyrinth, there can be few reasons for not becoming one of the millions of people who now regularly step onto its path.

May the paths that you walk be enriching ones, and may the labyrinth open up more of its mysteries to you as you discover its many gifts.

Labyrinth A-Ω

Notes and References

[1] in *Labyrinths: Ancient Paths of Wisdom and Peace*, Virginia Westbury, 2001, Aurum Press Ltd, p. 7.

[2] *Through the Labyrinth: Designs and Meanings over 5000 Years*, Hermann Kern, 1982, Prestel Press, New York, p. 23.

[3] 'Is That a Fact?', Jeff Saward & Kimberly Lowelle Saward, originally published in *Caerdroia* 33, 2003, pp.14-28.

[4] Sacred geometry: giving critical or symbolic meaning in architecture and design to universal patterns found in Nature, geometric shapes, proportions, and alignment.

On the meaning of sacred geometry, Jim Buchanan (*Labyrinths for the Spirit: How to Create Your Own Labyrinths for Meditation and Enlightenment*, 2007, Gaia, p. 97) suggests that Christian numerology lies at the heart of the design of the Chartres labyrinth: it splits into four quadrants (representing the four Gospels and four stages of Mass); we walk its eleven rings 'in sin', until we reach its center, or twelfth space (twelve being both the number of apostles, and the multiple of the numbers signifying the Masculine (3) and the Feminine (4)).

Sig Lonegren develops one aspect of this symbolism further, aligning the four stages of Mass with the processes of awakening (posing the question, 'when did I become aware of this?'), sacrifice ('what will I have to do to resolve it?'), transubstantiation (change), and culmination ('what will it look like when I've made this change?') (*Labyrinths: Ancient Myths and Modern Uses*, Sig. Lonegren, 2007, Gothic Image, p. 149).

In *Labyrinths, Their Geomancy and Symbolism*, Nigel Pennick (*Labyrinths, Their Geomancy and Symbolism*, Nigel Pennick, 1984, Runestaff pp. 16-17) also comments on the numerology of the design of labyrinths found in Christian settings, remarking that written into these are "the balance of male and female, between Christ and Lucifer, and the symbolism of man's life of 'three score years and ten'".

[5] Hermann Kern, quoted in *Labyrinths, Walking Toward the Center*, Gernot Candolini, 2001, Crossroads, p. 141.

[6] Maia Scott traces the history of Italian labyrinths in 'The Labyrinth, a Continued Italian Legacy', *The Spirit of Veriditas, Voices From The Labyrinth*, Winter 2009, p. 10.

[7] Geomancy is described by author Philip Carr-Gomm (*The Elements of the Druid Tradition*, Philip Carr-Gomm, Element, 1991, p. 96) as "the art and science which determines the correct siting of temples, sacred circles, tombs and monuments in relation to the forces of heaven and earth. It is a knowledge of the sacredness of the earth. One of its basic

tenets is that the Earth carries currents of vital energy which flow in lines, just as the body carries currents of subtle energy, known to the Chinese acupuncturists as Ch'i".

[8] Candolini, 2001, *op. cit.*, p. 51

[9] *Walking a Sacred Path: Rediscovering the Labyrinth as a Spiritual Practice*, Lauren Artress, 2006, Riverhead, New York, p. 20.

[10] Artress, 2006, *ibid.*, p. 157.

[11] Candolini, 2001, *op. cit.*, p. 30.

[12] Westbury, 2001, *op. cit.*, p. 13.

[13] Candolini, 2001, *op. cit.*, p. 55.

[14] See Lonegren, 2007, *op. cit.*

[15] Westbury, 2001, *op. cit.*, p.14.

[16] Lonegren, 2007, *op. cit.*, p. 3.

[17] While accurate monitoring of brainwaves is difficult, an increasing number of studies of changing brainwave patterns during sleep or meditation have been undertaken. See, for example, http://www.brainworksneurotherapy.com/what-are-brainwaves.

[18] *Walking the Path to Tomorrow Together or Reconciling Inner and Outer Journeys*, Clare Wilson, www.peacesanctuary.org, accessed 24 January 2017.

[19] *Steps Toward Common Ground, The Labyrinth's Role in Building Beloved Community* (Doctor of Ministry Thesis), Rev. Kathryn A. McLean, Chicago, Illinois, May 2016, p. 17.

[20] *And by our hands.... The La Falda Labyrinth*, Judith Tripp, http://circleway.com, accessed 18 January 2017.

[21] 'Labyrinth Prayers for Healing in Myanmar', Jill Geoffrion, *Labyrinth Pathways* (3) July 2009, pp. 8-12.

[22] 'Labyrinths, Spirituality & Quality of Life', Bob Gordon, *Labyrinth Pathways* (3) , July 2009, pp. 13-15.

[23] *Magical Paths: Labyrinths and Mazes in the 21st Century*, Jeff Saward, 2002, Mitchell Beasley (Octopus), London p. 205.

[24] 'Commonly Reported Effects of Labyrinth Walking', John D. Rhodes *Labyrinth Pathways* (2) July 2008 pp. 31-37.

[25] Geoffrion, July 2009, *op. cit.*, p. 11.

[26] *Labyrinth Pathways* (10) Sep 2016, The Labyrinth in a Residential Treatment Center, Charles Gillispie , pp. 26-31.

[27] http://www.sydneylabyrinth.org/about/, accessed 14 January 2017.

[28] *Breathe, You Are Alive: The Sutra on the Full Awareness of Breathing*, Thich Nhat Hanh, 1992, Rider.

[29] 'Intuipath® Finger labyrinth and Brain Synchrony', interview with Neal Harris by Tina Christensen, *Labyrinths Matter Newsletter* (5), May 2016, pp. 2-5.

[30] in Candolini, 2001, *op. cit.* p. 9.

Bibliography

The following bibliography illustrates the varied scope of the many excellent publications that might be consulted by anyone interested in deepening their knowledge about labyrinths. This list is by no means exhaustive.

Labyrinthos offers an extensive bibliography via its website, www.labyrinthos.net/bibliography.html, including titles relating to specialist areas of interest.

Canvas Labyrinths Construction Manual by Robert Ferré, 2014, Labyrinth Enterprises

Chartres Cathedral by Malcolm Miller, 1997, 2nd edition, Riverside Book Co

Christian Prayer And Labyrinths: Pathways to Faith, Hope, and Love by Jill Kimberly Hartwell Geoffrion, 2004, Pilgrim Press, Cleveland

The Healing Labyrinth: Finding Your Path to Inner Peace by Helen Raphael Sands, 2001, Barron's Educational Series

Kids on the Path, School Labyrinth Guide by Marge McCarthy, Labyrinth Resource Group http://labyrinthresourcegroup.org/wp-content/uploads/2012/03/kids_on_the_path_-part_1.pdf (supported by a DVD)

Laberintos: tradición viva (Sapere Aude) de Fernando Segismundo Alonso Garzón, 2014, masonica.es (En español / in Spanish)

Labyrinths: Ancient Myths and Modern Uses by Sig Lonegren, 2015, Gothic Image Publications, Glastonbury

The Labyrinth and the Enneagram, Circling into Prayer by Jill Kimberly Hartwell Geoffrion and Elizabeth Catherine Nagel, 2001, Pilgrim Press, Cleveland

Labyrinth: Landscape of the Soul by Di Williams, 2011, Wild Goose, Glasgow

Labyrinths and Mazes: A Complete Guide to Magical Paths of the World by Jeff Saward, 2003, Lark Books (Sterling), New York, and Gaia Books (Octopus), London

Labyrinth Reflections by Cathy Rigali and Lorraine Villemaire, http://www.labyrinthreflections.com/order

The Labyrinth Revival: A Personal Account by Robert Ferré, 1996, 2nd edition, Labyrinth Enterprises, LLC

Labyrinths for the Spirit: How to Create Your own Labyrinth for Meditation and Enlightenment by Jim Buchanan, 2006, Sterling Publishing Co., Distributed by Gaia Books, New York

Labyrinths, Walking Toward the Center by Gernot Candolini, 2001, Crossroads, New York

Labyrinth Journeys: 50 States, 51 Stories by Twylla Alexander, 2017, Springhill Publishing, the story of Twylla's labyrinth pilgrimage around the USA

Little Miracles on the Path: 20 Labyrinth Stories Celebrating 20 Years of Veriditas, www.veriditas.org/books

Living the Labyrinth by Jill K.G. Geoffrion, 2000, Pilgrim Press, Cleveland

The Magical Labyrinth by Ruth Weaver, 2013 Preschool - Kindergarten (for children)

Magical Paths: Labyrinths & Mazes in the 21st Century by Jeff Saward 2002, Mitchell Beasley (Octopus), London

The Magic of Labyrinths by Liz Simpson, 2002, Thorsons

The Mysteries of Chartres Cathedral by Louis Charpentier, 1972 Rilko Books, Rye

The Sacred Path Companion: A Guide to Walking the Labyrinth to Heal and Transform by Lauren Artress, 2006, Riverhead, New York

Steps Along an Unfolding Path: A Journey through Life and Labyrinths by Lars Howlett, 2011, biomorphic.org

Through the Labyrinth: Designs and Meanings over 5000 Years by Hermann Kern, 1982, Prestel Press, New York

Walking a Sacred Path: Rediscovering the Labyrinth as a Spiritual Practice by Lauren Artress, 2006, Riverhead, New York

The Way of the Labyrinth: A Powerful Meditation for Everyday Life by Helen Curry, 2000, Penguin Books, New York

Way of the Winding Path: A Map for the Labyrinth of Life by M. A. Eve Eschner Hogan, 2003, White Cloud Press

Working with the Labyrinth by Ruth Sewell, Jan Sellers & Di Williams, 2013, Wild Goose Publications

Journals

Caerdroia. The Journal of Mazes and Labyrinths. Research relating to the study labyrinths and mazes, published annually. http://www.labyrinthos.net/caerdroia.html

Labyrinths Matter Newsletter from the Australian Labyrinth Network.

Labyrinth Network North West Newsletter www.labyrinthnetworknorthwest.org/newsletters/2010/100423_LNN_Newsletter.pdf

Labyrinth Pathways. published annually by Labyrinthos (also available to Labyrinth Society members). www.labyrinthos.net

Little Miracles on the Path. Monthly inspirational stories from labyrinth experiences, produced by Linda Mikel. www.veriditas.org

The Labyrinth Journal. (copies available up to Winter 2012) www.veriditas.org/journal

TLS Members e-Newsletter. Quarterly newsletter for members of The Labyrinth Society.

DVD's

Rediscovering the Labyrinth: A Walking Meditation with Lauren Artress, Grace Cathedral, San Francisco

Labyrinths For Our Time: Places of Refuge in a Hectic World, The Labyrinth Society

Pathway to Change: Jail Labyrinth Project by Lorraine Villemaire and Cathy Rigali

The Troy Ride - A Labyrinth for Horses by Cordelia Rose & Ben Nicholson (other DVD's featuring horses, healing, and the labyrinth are available from Whitewater Mesa Labyrinths, www.wmlabyrinths.com).

Clive Johnson

The Labyrinth Resources Guide

Societies, membership bodies, and centers for labyrinth research

The Labyrinth Society. Worldwide organization, whose members include labyrinth makers, labyrinth facilitators, and anyone having an interest in or an appreciation for labyrinths. Members also have access to an archive of journal articles, and can enjoy a lively exchange of views on everything relating to labyrinths via the Society's Facebook group. www.labyrinthsociety.org

Veriditas. Provides training and accreditation for labyrinth facilitators. Encourages best practice for labyrinth hosting and promotes the benefits of labyrinth walking. www.veriditas.org

Labyrinthos. The research body and center of information on the labyrinth's history, purpose, and application. Publishes the annual journal Labyrinth Pathways (also available to Labyrinth Society members). www.labyrinthos.net

The Labyrinth Coalition. Resource, networking, and events coordinator, focusing on the US Midwest. www.labyrinths.org

The Labyrinth Guild of New England. New England based community of labyrinth aficionados, facilitators, and event organizers. www.labyrinthguild.org

Labyrinth Link Australia. www.labyrinthlinkaustralia.org

Labyrinth Network Northwest (serving the Pacific Northwest). www.labyrinthnetworknorthwest.org

Online forums, blogs, and social media

https://www.facebook.com/labyrintharoundamerica/ Labyrinth Around America Facebook page.

https://www.facebook.com/LabyrinthSociety/

www.facebook.com/veriditas.labyrinth

Labyrinth A-Ω

www.facebook.com/LabyrinthosUK

www.facebook.com/labyrinthwellnessllc

www.facebook.com/Labyrinthing

www.facebook.com/Labyrinthireland-156708794360950

https://labyrintharoundamerica.wordpress.com/ Labyrinth Around America blog.

www.blogmymaze.wordpress.com

https://guerrillalabyrinths.wordpress.com/labyrinth-blog

http://labyrinthos.blog/

http://labyrinthyoga.com/blog

https://www.instagram.com/thelabyrinthsociety/

https://twitter.com/LabyrinthSoc

https://twitter.com/labyrinthwisdom

https://www.linkedin.com/in/veriditas-inc-8157019a

Labyrinth locators

www.labyrinthlocator.com. The World-Wide Labyrinth Locator. Extensive online search facility for locating a labyrinth. Sponsored by The Labyrinth Society and Veriditas, Inc. through a generous grant from the Faith, Hope and Love Foundation. Researched and administered by Jeff Saward, a leading authority on the history and development of labyrinths and mazes, founding editor of Caerdroia – the Journal of Mazes and Labyrinths, and co-founder and director of Labyrinthos.

www.labyrinths.org. The Labyrinth Coalition's directory of labyrinths.

www.labyrinthlinkaustralia.org/labyrinth_directory.htm. An interactive map of labyrinths in Australia.

www.labyrinthnetworknorthwest.org/. (Pacific Northwest)

www.paxworks.com/labguy/hospitallinks.html. Links to hospital labyrinths.

Facilitators and labyrinth hire

www.veriditas.org. Veriditas' 'Find a Facilitator' directory. Advanced search facility for finding a Veriditas trained facilitator.

www.labyrinths.org/lablocators.html. The Labyrinth Coalition's directory of facilitators.

www.labyrinthguild.org. (Boston, MA area)

Portable labyrinth makers

Note: Most suppliers in this and the following sections will ship products / offer their services worldwide.

www.discoverlabyrinths.com. Discover Labyrinths LLC (USA)

www.labyrinthbuilders.co.uk. The Labyrinth Builders (UK)

www.labyrinthcompany.com. The Labyrinth Company (USA)

www.labyrinth-enterprises.com. Labyrinth Enterprises, LLC (USA)

www.pathsofpeace.com. Paths of Peace, the maker of the labyrinth for Labyrinth Around America. (USA)

www.paxworks.com. Paxworks (USA)

www.robinmcgauley.com. Robin McGauley (Canada)

www.veriditas.org/canvaslabyrinth. Veriditas (USA)

Permanent labyrinth constructors and consultants

www.pathsofpeace.com. Paths of Peace (USA)

www.labyrinthbuilders.co.uk. The Labyrinth Builders (UK)

www.labyrinthcompany.com. The Labyrinth Company (USA)

www.labyrinthireland.com. labyrinthireland.com. Design advice, facilitation, and workshops (Ireland)

http://www.labyrinthos.net/construction.html. Labyrinthos. Design, advice, publications and tours. (UK)

www.labyrinths.com.au. Mark Healy Labyrinths (Australia)

www.labyrinthsinstone.com. Labyrinths In Stone (USA)

www.veriditas.org/construction. Veriditas (USA)

'Pop-up' labyrinth suppliers

www.discoverlabyrinths.com. Discover Labyrinths. Quick and easy labyrinth construction for community and other events by Lars Howlett. (USA)

www.labyrinthsociety.org/make-a-labyrinth. Directions on how to make a labyrinth from The Labyrinth Society.

The Sand Labyrinth Kit by Lauren Artress, 2002, Tuttle Publications. Includes a book, two templates, and a bag of sand. www.veriditas.org

www.asacredjourney.net/2015/11/make-your-own-labyrinth. Journey Book Club article describing three ways to make your own labyrinth.

www.centerforfaithandhealth.org/resources. Center for Faith and Hope. Offers guidance on how to create a labyrinth.

Geomancy consultants

www.bouldermasterbuilders.com. BoulderMasterBuilders / Dominique Susani, internationally acclaimed geomancer and labyrinth builder. (France)

www.landandspirit.net. Land and Spirit (UK)

www.markopogacnik.com. Marko Pogačnik, internationally acclaimed geomancer and UNESCO Artist for Peace. (Slovenia)

www.geomancy.org. Mid Atlantic Geomancy by Avalon in Holland, Sig Lonegren, lifelong geomancer and founding member of The Labyrinth Society (Netherlands)

www.richardfeatheranderson.com/American_School_of_Geomancy.html. American School of Geomancy (USA)

Finger labyrinth suppliers

www.dasfingerlabyrinth.com/kaufen-2. Das Fingerlabyrinth (Germany)

www.dmhstudio.com. DMH Studio. (also offers guidance on how to make a finger labyrinth) (USA)

www.escapepathllc.com. E.S.C.A.P.E. PATH (USA)

https://goo.gl/bUpvoE. Veriditas Chartres Labyrinth (USA)

www.harmonylabyrinths.com. Harmony Labyrinths (USA)

www.ispiritual.com. iSpiritual.com (USA)

www.labyrinths.com.au. Mark Healy Labyrinths (Australia)

www.labyrinthshop.com. The Labyrinth Shop (USA)

www.mindfulsoulutions.ca. Mindful Soulutions (Canada)

www.mountainvalleycenter.com/labyrinth-gifts.php. Mountain Valley Center (USA)

www.pathsofpeace.com. Paths of Peace (USA)

www.paxworks.com. Paxworks (USA)

www.pilgrimpaths.co.uk. Pilgrim Paths Ltd (UK)

www.qdimensions.com.au. QDimensions (Australia)

www.relax4life.com/index.html. Relax4Life (USA)

www.robinmcgauley.com. Robin McGauley (Canada)

Free pattern for crocheting/knitting a finger labyrinth

http://www.welcatg.org/filebin/PDF/Labyrinth_FINAL.pdf. Women of the ELCA (Online), includes helpful factsheet and instructions on how to use the labyrinth

Facilitator training

www.veriditas.org. Veriditas, the principal accrediting body for labyrinth facilitators. (USA and worldwide)

www.labyrinthjourney.com/index.asp. Labyrinth-Journey (USA)

Labyrinth museums

www.butterflyzoo.co.uk. Puzzle Maze, Symonds Yat, Herefordshire, UK. A small museum tracing the history of labyrinths and mazes.

Labyrinth cards

www.helenwilltheartofhealing.com. The Art of Healing (Canada). Beautifully drawn card decks for use in walking meditation.

www.labyrinthwisdom.com. Labyrinth Wisdom Cards (Ireland). Offers a 48 card deck and handbook, illustrating labyrinths and posing questions for reflection.

Resources to download

https://zdi1.zd-cms.com/cms/res/files/382/labyrinth_proposal_template-1.pdf. Template Proposal for a community or institutional labyrinth project. (The Labyrinth Society)

https://zdi1.zd-cms.com/cms/res/files/382/ChartresLabyrinth.pdf. Chartres Labyrinth Drawing.

http://www.labyrintharoundamerica.net/Labyrinth_Walk_Handout_v01.pdf. Labyrinth Around America pre-walk handout (English).

http://www.labyrintharoundamerica.net/Labyrinth_Walk_HandoutES_v01.pdf. Labyrinth Around America folleto de pre-paseo (Spanish).

www.centerforfaithandhealth.org/resources. Center for Faith and Hope. Offers templates for creating paper labyrinths.

Other helpful sources for finding out about labyrinths

www.art.tfl.gov.uk/labyrinth. A fascinating survey of a major artwork for London's Underground system by Mark Wallinger, which involved installing labyrinth artwork at each of the Tube's 270 stations.

Clive Johnson

www.cathedrale-chartres.org/en/,251.html. Chartres Cathedral Labyrinth, Chartres, France

www.centennialparklands.com.au. Sydney Centennial Park Labyrinth, Sydney, Australia

www.gracecathedral.org/labyrinth. Grace Cathedral, San Francisco

www.graceinhouston.org/visiting-joining/tree-of-life-labyrinth. 'Tree of Life' labyrinth, Grace Episcopal Church, Houston, Texas

www.labyrintharoundamerica.net. Labyrinth Around America. Home of the project of the same name to take a labyrinth around the border states of the continental USA. Created and maintained by Clive Johnson, author of this book. Supported by a Facebook page, https://www.facebook.com/labyrintharoundamerica/, and a blog, https://labyrintharoundamerica.wordpress.com.

www.labyrinthos.net. Labyrinthos. Offers a wide range of information on the history and mysteries of labyrinths, including an extensive bibliography and guides to labyrinths in various countries.

www.labyrinths.org/resources/worldpeace-labyrinth05.pdf. World Peace Labyrinth

https://labyrinthsociety.org/tls-365-experience. **The 365 Experience offers daily experiences** on The Labyrinth Society's Facebook page and website for anyone to consider, contemplate and use, with contributions from TLS members (no access to a labyrinth of your own is necessary to enjoy taking part).

www.labyrinthsociety.org/labyrinths-in-places. Labyrinths in Places offers a range of resources and guidance for individuals or groups considering introducing labyrinths into different contexts (including schools, churches, prisons, counseling sessions, retreats, public parks, and colleges and universities).

www.lessons4living.com/labyrinth.htm. General resources.

www.reconciliationlabyrinth.withtank.com. The Reconciliation Labyrinth, South Africa

www.ssqie.com. Sacred Sites Quest. Gives students exposure to diverse cultures, often involving community labyrinth projects. See also Reginald Adams' own website at www.reginaldadams.com.

YouTube and online videos

www.youtube.com/channel/UCvlZ0FybLM_mqho-HlT1Nqow. Dedicated YouTube channel of The

Labyrinth Society, includes videos on various topics, e.g. labyrinth uses in churches (www.youtube.com/watch?v=6wB19SPNBQg), prisons (www.youtube.com/watch?v=W2uBjA4za-I), and schools (www.youtube.com/watch?v=hkbtv2QR3IA).

www.youtube.com/watch?v=o7u80ZLEh3M Labyrinth History & Walking by The Labyrinth Society

www.youtube.com/watch?v=shpJpL9SKXM Labyrinth - A Walking Meditation by Tori Fiore Film Projects

www.youtube.com/watch?v=ZUXQBxElRWY How to make a Quilted Finger Labyrinth by Women of the ELCA

www.youtube.com/watch?v=WJ6J2Haktdc Walking Meditation: Grace Cathedral Labyrinth by Kirsten Johnson

www.labyrinthsociety.org/labyrinth-types. Labyrinth Types - A Guide to the Many Kinds of Labyrinths Found all over the World by The Labyrinth Society

https://www.youtube.com/watch?v=SX_orvEelak. Leaf Labyrinth by Discover Labyrinths. Stephen Shibley and Lars Howlett show how to make a labyrinth using fallen leaves.

www.youtube.com/watch?v=f9rt39ieP5E. Lauren Artress on the Labyrinth by Bob Hughes

http://art.tfl.gov.uk/labyrinth/about. About Labyrinth by Mark Wallinger. The artist responsible for bringing labyrinth artwork to the London Underground system talks about this inspiring project.

www.youtube.com/watch?v=i33t89tnGfU. Creating a Masking Tape Labyrinth by Warren Lynn

www.youtube.com/watch?v=7TjEo6y1_eY. Finger Walking the Chartres Labyrinth Board

www.youtube.com/watch?v=jXluF1x1sbo. Healing powers of Labyrinths explained and experienced by Lilou Mace

www.youtube.com/watch?v=I4jyt8KJyYw. A Bit of Labyrinth History by Guideposts

www.youtube.com/watch?v=DgYTwmgGsJc. Labyrinth Locations by The Labyrinth Society

www.youtube.com/watch?v=1aMAuekhi_A. The Search for Meaning in the Labyrinth of Life - Lauren Artress and Phil Cousineau by VeriditasWebVideos www.youtube.com/watch?v=ik1TdDNKfE8. Sacred Sites Quest Ecuador 2017: Promotional video by Reginald Adams

www.youtube.com/watch?v=_GE-UBdXbrg How to Make your own Plaster Finger Labyrinth by Lise Lotz

Podcasts

www.labyrinthsociety.org/media/categories/1708-podcasts. Extensive and growing range of podcasts from The Labyrinth Society.

www.abc.net.au/local/stories/2015/10/08/4326896.htm. Interview with Jo Cook, founder of the Tasmanian Recovery From Eating Disorders group. Jo's encounter with the labyrinth helped her to overcome her recovery from an eating disorder.

www.abc.net.au/radionational/programs/breakfast/the-labyrinth/2992930. ABC Radio National *RN Breakfast* interview with Rev. Dr Lauren Artress.

www.abc.net.au/radionational/programs/spiritofthings/ladies--of-the--labyrinth/6127862. *The Spirit of Things*, 'Ladies of the labyrinth'. Inspiring ABC Radio National interview with Lauren Artress and Emily Simpson, whose vision and commitment led to the creation of the Sydney Centennial Park labyrinth.

www.bestofbcb.org/out-002-landscape-artist-describes-his-labyrinth-in-serene-park/. Bainbridge Community Broadcasting interview with Jeffrey Bales, creator of a community-based stone-surface labyrinth.

www.labyrintharoundamerica.com/LaACJph.mp3. Clive Johnson talks about the inspiration for and intention of the Labyrinth Around America project.

http://www.onbeing.org/program/the-science-of-healing-places/4856. *On Being with Krista Tippett*, 'Esther Sternberg – The Science of Healing Places'. Includes reflections on the benefits of labyrinths as healing spaces.

Clive Johnson

ACKNOWLEDGEMENTS

My thanks are due to all the teachers, supporters, and fellow walkers who have helped me on my labyrinth journey; to TJ, the ever-patient and loyal collie who sat by my side during most of my writing; to Monica Douglas-Clark for her excellent proof reading; and to The Great Divine–The Creator and Keeper of the labyrinth's mysteries.

Clive Johnson

ABOUT THE AUTHOR

Clive Johnson is a Veriditas trained labyrinth facilitator, interfaith minister, and labyrinth enthusiast. This is his eighth book.

www.clivejohnson.info
www.clivejohnsonministry.com
www.labyrintharoundamerica.net

ALSO BY CLIVE JOHNSON:

Picturing God: How to conceive and relate to the Divine (An Anthology)
Fairy Stories & Fairy Stories: Traditional tales for children, Contemporary tales for adults
Arabian Nights & Arabian Nights: Traditional tales from a thousand and one nights, Contemporary tales for adults
The Complete Guide to Visioning: How to discover, shape and realize your vision

Coming soon:

Modern Spirituality for the Non-religious
Ceremonies for One
Interfaith: The Essential Beginners' Guide
Spiritual Practice A–Ω

Clive Johnson

Lightning Source UK Ltd.
Milton Keynes UK
UKHW010813130519
342574UK00016B/1220/P

9 780995 735101